DID Y

. . . the inspiration for the S_____?

. . . the Slinky faced much scorn and rejection before becoming the hit of the 1946 Toy Fair?

. . . Slinky sales have totaled more than 250 million? That's roughly one Slinky for every man, woman, and child in the United States?

. . . the Slinky has made numerous cameos in the movies and on television, yet remains as humble and down-to-earth as ever?

THE OFFICIAL
Slinky®
Book

Also by Joey Green

Polish Your Furniture with Panty Hose

Paint Your House with Powdered Milk

Wash Your Hair with Whipped Cream

Joey Green's Encyclopedia

The Bubble Wrap Book

The Zen of Oz

The Warning Label Book

Monica Speaks

THE OFFICIAL
Slinky®
Book

Hundreds of Wild and Wacky Uses for the Greatest Toy on Earth

Joey Green

This book is an original publication of The Berkley Publishing Group.

THE OFFICIAL SLINKY® BOOK

A Berkley Book / published by arrangement with the author

PRINTING HISTORY
Berkley trade paperback edition / October 1999

The Penguin Putnam Inc. World Wide Web site address is http://www.penguinputnam.com

ISBN 0-425-17155-8

BERKLEY®
Berkley Books are published by The Berkley Publishing Group, a division of Penguin Putnam Inc., 375 Hudson Street, New York, New York 10014.
BERKLEY and the "B" design are trademarks belonging to Penguin Putnam Inc.

PRINTED IN THE UNITED STATES OF AMERICA
10 9 8 7 6 5 4 3 2 1

For Slinky lovers everywhere.
May you forever spring forth.

What walks down stairs alone or in pairs
And makes a slinkity sound?
A spring, a spring, a marvelous thing,
Ev'ryone knows it's Slinky!

It's Slinky, Slinky!
For fun, it's a wonderful toy!
It's Slinky, it's Slinky!
It's fun for a girl and a boy!

Introduction

A SLINKY CAN BE ANYTHING you want it to be—a toy, an exercise machine, a stress-reliever, a television antenna, a physics project, a friend, a lover, or an improper relationship.

What explains the Slinky's enduring popularity? Its sheer simplicity? Or the fact that a Slinky has hundreds of practical uses? High school teachers use them to demonstrate the properties of waves. U.S. troops in Vietnam used them as mobile radio antennas by tossing them over tree branches. Pecan harvesters have used them in machinery to help collect pecans. Scientists use them to understand the supercoiling of DNA molecules. NASA has used them in zero-gravity physics experiments in the Space Shuttle.

Or could the Slinky's longevity be attributed to the fact that this versatile spring toy doesn't come with instructions to hamper your creativity? You can do anything you want with a Slinky. So let's stretch the limits of our imaginations and spring into action!

—Joey Green

Poor Man's Slinky

Can't afford a Slinky of your own?

If you look at the bottom right-hand corner of each odd-numbered page in this book, you'll notice a drawing of a Slinky. If you flip the pages slowly, the Slinky will walk across the bottom of the book.

On the bottom of each even-numbered page you'll find a drawing of a Slinky stretched across the page. Flip the pages of the book slowly and you'll see a longitudinal wave travel back and forth across the Slinky coil.

The Miracle of the Slinky

As WORLD WAR II RAGED IN 1943, RICHARD JAMES, A TWENTY-NINE-year-old marine engineer working in Philadelphia's Cramp Shipyard, tried to figure out how to use springs to mount delicate meters for testing horsepower on battleships. A torsion spring fell off his desk and tumbled end over end across the floor. Convinced he could devise a steel formula that would give the spring the right tension to "walk," Richard brought the spring home to his wife, Betty, and said, "I think I can make a toy out of this."

After Richard found a steel wire that would coil, uncoil, and recoil, Betty thumbed through the dictionary to find an appropriate name for the toy. She chose Slinky because it meant "stealthy, sleek, and sinuous." Richard began thinking of marketing his toy. But manufacturers told him he couldn't expect to sell an unpainted spring as a toy. The Navy also took no interest in Richard's springs.

In the summer of 1945, Richard finally found a machine shop that would manufacture the $2\frac{1}{2}$-inch stack of ninety-eight coils. The Jameses borrowed five hundred dollars to pay the company to make a small quantity of Slinkys. They tried to sell the toy through retail stores in Philadelphia. But without any name recognition, the springs didn't jump off the shelves.

Desperate to cash in on the Christmas season, the Jameses talked a buyer from Gimbel's Department Store in downtown Philadelphia into providing counter space for four hundred Slinkys and letting them demonstrate the Slinky to customers. Richard James went alone, carrying a small demonstration staircase with him. Fearing that no one would buy the Slinky because it was so simple, Richard slipped a dollar bill to a friend to make sure at least one Slinky was sold. But that night, all four hundred Slinkys sold in ninety minutes.

The Slinky became the hit of the 1946 American Toy Fair, and Slinky sales soared. Richard James quit his job at the shipyard to devote all his energy to the Slinky. Betty used to take the day's production home at night and hand-wrap the Slinkys in yellow paper. The Jameses founded James Industries with a factory in Philadelphia to market their product. Richard invented machines that could coil eighty feet of steel wire into a Slinky in less than eleven seconds. That same year, the Jameses started running commercials in the fledgling television industry, using local personalities like Miss Patty on *Romper Room*. In 1950, the Jameses introduced the compact Slinky Junior.

Then, in 1960, the Slinky story got even slinkier. Richard dramatically lost interest and abandoned both business and family to join a religious cult in Bolivia (he died there in 1974), leav-

ing Betty behind with six kids, a floundering business, and a huge debt (largely rung up by her husband's donations to his spiritual leaders). But just like the Slinky itself, Betty bounced back, relocating the factory to her hometown of Hollidaysburg, Pennsylvania, a small town near Altoona. Betty engineered the Slinky's comeback with a unique co-op advertising plan and a simple jingle that infected the collective consciousness of the Baby Boom.

The original Slinky has seen only two changes over the years. The prototype blue-black Swedish steel was replaced with less expensive, silvery American metal (specially coated for durability), and in 1973, the Slinky's ends were crimped for safety reasons. The Slinky is still made on Richard James's original machines in Hollidaysburg. And at two dollars, a Slinky costs only twice as much as it did more than fifty years ago. In 1979, the company introduced the plastic Slinky (in two colors), followed by the plastic Slinky Jr. The company also made several pull toys with Slinkys for bodies.

Betty ran the company until 1998 when, at the age of eighty-three, she sold James Industries to Poof Products so she would have more time to spend with her six children and sixteen grandchildren. Betty attributes the Slinky's success to one thing. "Its simplicity. . . . Children are intrigued by the sound and its walking down the stairs. The younger ones can't figure out what it's doing, and the older ones just like doing it."

"If you live in a house with steps, it can outlast most presents," explains Joanne Oppenheim, author of *The Best Toys, Books and Videos for Kids*. "It can be whatever a kid wants it to be, and the best toys are like that."

Wild and Wacky Uses for the Greatest Toy on Earth

Hat Security System

Prevent your hat from flying off your head in
the wind. Simply attach a Slinky inside the hat
and then strap the Slinky to the top of your
head. Should a gust of wind blow your hat off
your head, the Slinky will spring your hat right
back.

Squirrel Slink-Away

Prevent squirrels from climbing up the pole to
a bird feeder. Secure a Slinky to the bottom
of the bird feeder and let it hang down the
pole.

Slinky Burglar Alarm

Hang several Slinkys inside your
doors and windows. Should a crook
break into your house, the clanging
springs will wake you up so you
can dial 911.

Slink Shrink

Bouncing a Slinky between two hands relieves stress, springing tension away.

Slinky Jewelry

Wear a Slinky around your wrist just as you would wear bangles.

Suspenders

Crisscross two Slinkys and wear them as suspenders, not simply to keep your pants from falling down, but to make everyone in the office sit up and take notice of your chic attire.

Slinky the Ferret

If you have a pet ferret, let the long, slim weasel climb through your Slinky. Ferrets love gliding through the springy coils, which could explain why so many pet ferrets are named Slinky.

Slinky Fact

Slinky sales have totaled
more than 250 million.
That's roughly one Slinky for
every man, woman, and child
in the United States.

Hypnosis Slinky

If you're a hypnotist, you can swing a Slinky to put your patients into a hypnotic trance.

Instant Slinky Antenna

Using a wire with an alligator clip, attach a Slinky to your television or radio, and then stretch the Slinky across the room to improve your reception.

Slinky Beer Caddie

Set your beer can inside a Slinky. Emily Post, look out!

Practical Jokers!

They'll think the bed is defective if you cut a small hole in the center of a mattress, slip a few coils of a Slinky inside the bed, and stretch the remaining coils over the edge of the mattress.

Move Over, Martha Stewart

Attach a Slinky to the ceiling just over the chandelier and let the Slinky drop down over the chandelier chain for a touch of elegance.

Party Decoration

Instead of stringing crepe paper streamers around the room, drape Slinkys from corner to corner for a party they'll never forget.

Bowling Ball Holder

Set a Slinky on the table and set your bowling ball on top of it. It's not just practical. It's modern art!

Slinky Poker

Slip your poker hand into the coils of a Slinky to hold your cards in place.

THE OFFICIAL Slinky Book

Adorable

A Slinky makes a great door stop. Or if you don't want to keep the door open, use a Slinky to make a spring door that always stays shut.

Portable Clothesline

When camping, hang a Slinky between two trees to create a makeshift clothesline.

Lamp of the Future

Attach a Slinky to the top of the lamp fixture and let it drop over the lamp stand pole to create a lamp that looks like it's from the set of *Deep Space Nine*.

Let It Snow

Scrape the snow off your shoes on a snow scraper made by stretching a Slinky across the foot of your front door.

A Solve-It-Yourself Slinky Mystery

Standing on a ladder, hold a Slinky at one end, and let the other end hang down without touching the ground. When you drop the Slinky will the bottom end spring upward? Or will the bottom end fall to the ground first? Or will the bottom end stay where it is until the entire Slinky has collapsed and then fall to the ground?

Kitty Slink-Away

Keep cats off furniture by stretching a Slinky across your couch. This might also keep people off your couch, but you may consider that a side benefit.

Grand Old Slinky

Add a decorative touch to Old Glory by letting a Slinky hang over a flag pole.

Guess Who's Slinking to Dinner

Using a Slinky Junior as a napkin ring is sure to impress those all-important dinner guests.

Slinky in the Gutter

Keep leaves out of your rain gutters. Place a Slinky in your rain gutter and stretch it from one end to the next, keeping it in place by simply clipping the Slinky to each end.

Slinky Fact

An original blue-black 1945 Slinky is worth about $100 today. That's one hundred times its original price of one dollar.

Fa-La-La-La-La

Decorate a Christmas tree with a Slinky. You can wrap the tree in a Slinky and then hang Slinky Juniors as ornaments for the ultimate in tinsel.

La-La-La-La

And if you decorate your house in Christmas lights, why stop there? Drape Slinkys across your house and through the tress to really give your house some holiday spirit.

Up, Up, and Away

Tie six helium balloons to one end of a Slinky and sit the other end on the ground. The balloons will lift one end of the Slinky into the air, leaving the other end sitting as an anchor on the ground.

Slinky Ducts

Make flex tubing for conduits. Stretch a Slinky
from one duct to another and secure it in
place, then wrap plastic trash bags around the
coils, securing them in place with clear packaging
tape to make excellent ducting in a pinch.

Slinky Costume

Dress up for a costume party as a Slinky man or woman.
Wear a Slinky on each arm, securing one end of the Slinky
to your wrist, the other end at your shoulder. Fellow party-
goers will go wild for the chance to spring your coils.

Control Your Remote Control

Tired of losing the remote control to your
TV? Attach one end of a Slinky to the arm
rest of your couch and the other end to
your remote control so it always
springs back to its
proper place.

Slinky Fact

In 1999, the United States Postal Service introduced the world's first Slinky stamp.

The Wacky World of Waves

Using a Slinky you can learn the properties of waves. All you have to do is hold one end of the Slinky and have a partner hold the other end. Stretch the Slinky six feet between you. Then...

Make Transverse Waves

Move your hand up and down, and a wave will travel down the Slinky. This transverse wave is a model for electromagnetic waves such as light waves, water waves, and earthquake waves.

Make Horizontally Polarized Waves

When you move your hand from side to side, a wave travels down the Slinky. This is a horizontally polarized transverse wave.

Make Rotational Waves

When you move your hand up and down and side to side at the same time in a circle, a rotational wave travels down the Slinky. This wave is a model for circularly polarized light.

Make Circular Motion Waves

When you move your hand toward and away from you and up and down at the same time in a circle, a circular motion wave travels down the Slinky. This wave is a model for ocean waves and a type of earthquake wave called a love wave.

Make Torsional Waves

When you rotate your wrist, a torsional wave twists down the Slinky. This wave is a model for the waves that travel down violin strings.

Make Longitudinal Waves

When you move your hand toward and away from

you, a longitudinal wave travels down the Slinky. This wave (also known as a compression wave) is a model for sound waves in gases and liquids and for some earthquake waves.

(Another way to make a longitudinal wave is by having you and your partner stretch the Slinky six feet between you on the floor. Gather up a foot of coil, compress it in your hand, and release it.)

Make Rayleigh Waves

When you move your hand toward and away from you and side to side at the same time in a circle, a Rayleigh wave travels down the Slinky. This wave is a model for earthquake waves that travels through solids like the earth, but not through liquids and gases.

Close the Refrigerator

Attach one end of a Slinky to the inside back wall of your refrigerator and the other end to the inside of your refrigerator door to make your refrigerator self-closing.

Swing Time

Tired of having to push your child on the playground swing? Let the kid hold one end of a Slinky and attach the other end to a nearby tree. One push and the kid will be swinging forever.

The Ultimate Slinky Walk

Put a Slinky in an empty clothes dryer and turn it on, then watch the Slinky walk around the dryer as it spins. WARN-ING: This may heat up the Slinky to exceedingly hot temperatures, cause your dryer to catch fire, and burn down your house.

The Slinky in History #1

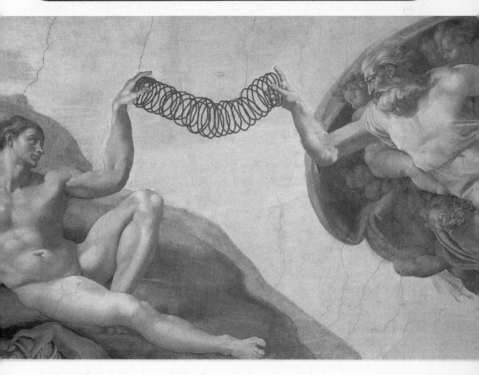

Michelangelo beautifully depicted the origins of the Slinky on the ceiling of the Sistine Chapel.

Stylish Shower Curtain

Slide a Slinky over your shower curtain rod and clip the shower curtain to the Slinky for a totally cool shower curtain that glides easily.

Christmas Stocking Stuffer

Put a Slinky inside your Christmas stocking to keep it wide open for even more goodies from Santa.

Spring Skiing

Have your runaway snow skis ever gone shooting down the mountain without you? Simply attach one end of a Slinky to the ski and the other end to your ski boot and you're skis will always land back on your feet.

Ski Pole Patrol

The only thing worse than losing your snow skis is losing your ski poles. Attach one end of a Slinky to your ski pole, the other end to the sleeve of your ski jacket. Now those poles will always be at your side.

Slinky Hollywood

- A Slinky can be seen descending a staircase in the hit film *Ace Ventura 2: When Nature Calls*.

- In the Disney movie *Inspector Gadget*, Inspector Gadget has Slinky parts.

- On television, the Slinky has made guest appearances on *Law and Order*, *Wings*, *This Could Be the Start of Something Big*, *Foul-ups, Bleeps and Blunders*, *Happy Days*, *St. Elsewhere*, *The Rosie O'Donnell Show*, and *Spin City*.

- The Slinky also made cameo appearances in the movies *Demolition Man*, John Waters's *Hairspray*, *The Inkwell*, *Other People's Money*, and *The Pink Panther*.

- Oddly, the Slinky did not play a part in the movie *Big*.

Rush Hour Woes

Keep a Slinky in your glove compartment so you've got something to do when stuck in bumper-to-bumper traffic. Or, use it to impress a cop when you're pulled over and asked to show your registration.

Earthquake Protection

Suspend valuables from the ceiling with a Slinky.

The Slinky Look

They'll flip when they see you descending the stairs in your Slinky dress.

The Slinky Walk

Find a board or table top with a non-slip surface. Place several books under one end of the board to slope the surface one foot for every four-foot length. Place the Slinky at the top, flip, and watch the Slinky walk down the board, end over end.

Slinky Dog

In 1952, seven years after the first Slinky appeared on the scene, Mrs. Helen Malsed of Seattle, Washington, sent an idea to Richard and Betty James. Later that year, Slinky Dog was on toy store shelves across America. Slinky Dog was eventually discontinued, but reappeared on the scene after he made a strong supporting role in the 1995 Disney movie *Toy Story* and the 1999 Disney sequel  *Toy Story 2.* The voice of Slinky Dog is provided by Jim Varney, better known as Ernest P. Worrell in the movies *Ernest Goes to Camp, Ernest Saves Christmas,* and *Ernest Goes to Jail.*

Slinky Baby-Sitter

Attach one end of the Slinky to a wall and the other end of the Slinky to the baby's foot. This way the baby can't crawl too far away without springing back into the family room.

Leave the Driving to Slinky

Attach Slinkys to the front and back bumpers of your car so the next time someone rear-ends your car, they'll spring back without harming your new paint job.

Basketball Slinky

Attach two Slinkys under each one of your sneakers so you can make incredible jump shots on the court and really put some spring into your step.

Handicapped Slinky

Got a broken leg? Wrap a Slinky around your cast several times so no one comes near you to bump into it.

A Slinky Moment

Comedian Steven Wright met his
girlfriend at Macy's.
"She was shopping," he explains. "I was
putting Slinkys on the escalator."

Poster Protector

Roll up that Keep On Truckin' black-light poster and insert it into a Slinky for safe keepin'.

Hail the Size of Slinkys

Protect your house from hail storms by covering your roof with Slinkys so the hail stones bounce right off, leaving your house untouched.

The Funky Slinky

To give your home that hipper-than-hip Studio 54–Danceteria-Sprockets nightclub look, hang Slinkys from the ceiling. And for an added touch, turn on the strobe light.

It's Curtains!

Hang Slinkys from the curtain rod to make sophisticated Slinky curtains for that trendy cosmopolitan look.

Slinky Fact

The Slinky jingle, broadcast on television continually since 1962, is one of the most well-known toy jingles in America, recognized by nearly 90 percent of all adults.

Slinky Fact

More than three million miles of wire have been used to make the classic Slinky since its inception. That's enough wire to make a Slinky big enough to hold the earth and stretch to the moon and back.

Let It All Hang Out

Hang several Slinkys over the door jamb and let them hang to the floor to create a funky variation on the Sixties beaded curtain.

Slinky Repellent

Prevent mosquito bites by slipping your arms and legs through Slinkys.

Slinky Disguise

Attach two Slinky Juniors to your eyeglasses with two plastic eyeballs to create eyeball glasses. Now they'll never know who you are in that police line-up.

Slinky Tires

What's worse than getting your car stuck in the snow in winter? Those clunky chains on your tires! Instead, wrap Slinkys around your tires for a hip look that's sure to make all your neighbors jealous.

Slinky in Space

Astronauts! Going for a space walk and afraid you'll float away into the inky blackness of space, never to be seen again? Secure yourself to the Mir Space Station with a Slinky so you always bounce back.

In Case of Emergency

Afraid to parachute out of an airplane but don't want everyone in your sky diving class to know? Attach yourself to the plane with a Slinky so you can jump out with everyone else, but bounce back before pulling your rip cord.

Slinky Drapery

Need to hold those new drapes in place? Use Slinkys as drapery holders.

Repel Pigeons

Having trouble with pigeons nesting under the eaves of your house? Stretch a Slinky across the spot and your troubles are gone.

An ancient Egyptian painting in the tomb of Sety I at Thebes shows the falcon-god Horus playing with a Slinky.

Slinky Facts

The word Slinky in Swedish translates to *traespiral*.

•

The Slinky is sold on every continent of the world except Antarctica.

How a Slinky Works

A Slinky is simply a large spring that stretches easily.

Like all objects, a Slinky has inertia. This means a Slinky at rest tends to stay at rest, and a Slinky in motion tends to stay in motion.

A Slinky sitting at the top of a staircase has *potential energy*. When a force is applied to the Slinky to make it start down the stairs, the Slinky is affected by gravity. The potential energy becomes *kinetic energy,* and the Slinky flips coil over coil down the stairs.

As the Slinky flips down the steps, the energy is transferred along its length in a compressional wave (resembling a sound wave).

How fast the Slinky moves depends upon the spring constant (the stiffness of the spring), the mass of the metal, the length of the Slinky, the diameter of the coils, and the height of the steps. This can be calculated using a tediously long mathematical equation that no one in their right mind cares to solve.

Hold the Mail

Stretch a Slinky across the table and use the coils to hold your mail or bills.

Slinky Bookends

Why keep your books in place with a boring bookend when you can use a Slinky to give your home or office a stylish designer look that's sure to make heads turn?

Earthquake Protection

Build your house on a foundation of Slinkys, so the next time there's seismic activity, your house will simply jiggle in place.

The Perfect Gift

Why throw away good money on a diamond engagement ring when you can give the gift that keeps on giving? After all, nothing says I love you quite like a Slinky.

Slinky Behind Bars

Is your loved one doing time? Bake a Slinky inside a cake. While there's no way to use a Slinky to break out of jail, the toy will give your incarcerated loved one hours of cell-time fun.

Totally Slinky, Dude!

Ever wipe out and lose your surfboard? Simply attach one end of a Slinky to the surfboard and wear the other end around your ankle, and that runaway surfboard will bounce right back before you can say "Cowabunga!"

The Slinky Has Landed

The real reason NASA stopped going to the moon was because the astronauts rebelled against all those bumpy landings on the moon's surface. Attaching a Slinky to the bottom of each foot of the Lunar Module would make those lunar landings smooth as silk and promptly revitalize interest in our moon program.

Slinky Boomerang

Tired of losing your boomerang? Attach it to a Slinky and the boomerang is guaranteed to return to you every time.

Bowling Ball Boomerang

Attach one end of a Slinky to your bowling ball, hold the free end of the Slinky, and toss your ball down the alley toward the pins. You'll never have to wait for that clunky old ball return to spit back your bowling ball again.

Slinky Wig

Attach two dozen Slinky Juniors to a bathing cap, and you've got a fashionable Slinky Wig.

Pomp and Slinky

A graduation cap covered with dangling Slinkys makes a poignant statement about the value of a college education that your university won't soon forget.

Slinky Lane

Make your neighborhood more contemporary
(and raise property values at the same time)
by hanging Slinkys from those tall street lamps
on your block.

Faulty Slinky

Filling the entire San Andreas Fault with Slinkys
could prevent a lot of damage during the
next earthquake (or maybe even stop the
Big One dead in its tracks).

Demolition Slinky

Weld one end of a Slinky to a
large steel ball and attach the
other end to the top of the
derrick on a crane to make
demolishing those buildings a
lot more unpredictable and exciting. Now you never know
what that ball will smash into next—giving you an excellent reason to wear a hard hat!

Here Comes the Slinky

Your family and friends will really spring into action when you walk down the aisle wearing a bridal gown made from Slinkys.

Order in the Court

Having trouble quieting your courtroom? Instead of banging a gavel, start playing with a Slinky to get everyone's undivided attention.

The Slinky Necklace

There's simply no need to buy expensive jewelry when you can wear an attractive Slinky around your neck that's sure to make you the talk of the town.

Elegant Earwear

And two Slinky Juniors make a set of luxurious hoop earrings and an unforgettable fashion statement.

The Slinky in History #3

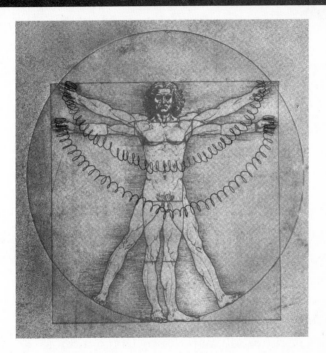

Renaissance artist Leonardo da Vinci, renowned for his in-depth study of human anatomy, also depicted the intricacies of a Slinky stretched from different angles.

Toilet Papering Substitute

Instead of toilet papering your neighbor's house, use Slinkys. It takes about 150 Slinkys to cover the house, cars, and trees, but the final result is well worth it.

Hard-Boiled Detective

It's easy to tell the difference between hard-boiled eggs and raw eggs in the refrigerator if each hard-boiled egg is sitting on top of its own Slinky Junior.

Spring Fashion

A Slinky necktie is something the ladies won't be able to resist. And if you're stuck in a boring meeting at work, you'll have something to keep you busy.

Tie One On!

Are your neckties all snarled up? Drape a Slinky across your closet and hang ties from the coils. What better way to keep your brand new Slinky tie from getting tangled?

Slinky Ping-Pong

Can't find the net for the Ping-Pong table?
Stretch a Slinky across the table and you're
ready to volley for serve.

Spring Fever?

In wintertime, hang Slinkys on the bare branches of trees.

Lunatic Fringe

Sew a Slinky along the bottom of your vest, jacket, shirt, or
handbag to create a funky Sixties fringe look.

Parking Lot Finder

Can't remember where you
parked? Hang a Slinky
down the length of
your car antenna so
you can always find
your car in the parking
lot. Bonus Tip: A Slinky

on your antenna will also improve your radio reception.

A Slinky Moment

In 1995, physicians at the University of Florida surgically implanted a tiny stretch of wire mesh resembling a Slinky into a bronchial tube of Edward Swift, a 63-year-old lung cancer patient, to open a severely blocked airway.

"I got immediate relief," said Swift. "It's a remarkable invention."

Slinky Barbie

Slip a naked Barbie doll into a Slinky to give
her a slinky dress Ken is sure to love.

Walk the Plank

Install a diving board so it tilts toward the swimming pool,
then make a Slinky walk down the plank into the pool and
let it sink to the bottom. WARNING: Although you may be
tempted to use a plastic Slinky for this trick to avoid rust-
ing a metal Slinky, please be advised that a plastic Slinky
will not satisfactorily sink to the bottom of a pool.

Psychedelic Slinky

Hold one end of a Slinky at chin level, drop the other end
to the floor, look down through the center of the Slinky,
and send waves bouncing up and down the coils for a
hypnotic view that would send Timothy Leary into a tizzy.

Detain a Criminal

Can't find rope or duct tape? Tie up a burglar by tangling
up a Slinky, then call 911.

The Wacky World of Centrifugal Force

If you hold one end of a Slinky and whirl it around your head, it swings out from you. This is caused by centrifugal force. The faster you make the Slinky go around, the longer the centrifugal forces stretches out the Slinky and raises it from the floor.

Slinky on the Hood

Using a blowtorch and wearing protective
goggles and gloves, weld a Slinky to the hood
of your car to make a hood ornament worthy
of a Bentley.

Barbed Wire Substitute

In a pinch, you can use a Slinky as barbed wire by simply
stretching it across the top of a fence or a fox hole. To
make prickly barbs, just adhere thumbtacks all over the
coils (stick-side out) with Krazy Glue.

Automatic Garage Door

Can't afford an electric garage
door opener? Attach one end
of a Slinky to the ceiling and
the other end to the inside
bottom of your garage door. Now
one touch will lift it open. WARNING:
Using more than one Slinky may make
closing the garage door a physical impossibility.

Slinky Facts

Neiman-Marcus sells a gold Slinky with an oak case for $80.

•

A Slinky is on exhibit in the Smithsonian Institute and in the Metropolitan Museum of Art.

Jumbo Pen Spring

Did you lose the spring inside a ballpoint pen made for the Jolly Green Giant? Never fear! A Slinky makes a great replacement!

Car Tow Thrill-ride

If you keep a Slinky in your glove compartment, there's no need ever to call AAA. Have another driver tow your car by attaching a Slinky to the back of his car or truck and then securing the other end of the Slinky to the front bumper of your car. When the vehicle in front moves forward, the Slinky will stretch, causing the car in back to careen into the front car, sending it flying forward.

Kid Leash

Tired of losing your small one in the mall? Keep your kid in tow by attaching one end of a Slinky to your child while you hold the other end. If your tyke wanders too far away, the Slinky will spring the adventurous toddler back to your side.

WARNING

■ Never use a Slinky as a leash for an elephant, hippopotamus, or rhinoceros.

■ Never rewire your home with a Slinky.

■ Never stretch a Slinky across the street in the hope that oncoming cars will be catapulted backward.

■ Never use a Slinky as a tail for your kite during a lightning storm.

■ Never permit a plastic surgeon to use Slinkys in lieu of silicone implants.

■ Never use a Slinky as a finish line for a marathon or a stock-car race.

Dog Leash

Why enroll Rover in obedience school? Attach one end of a Slinky to your dog's collar while you hold the other end. If your dog wanders too far, he'll spring right back to your side. Now you have a genuine Slinky dog that heels all by himself.

Back-up Curlers

If a hot date is about to ring your doorbell and you can't find your hair curlers, use a Slinky as a substitute. It's guaranteed to give your ringlets plenty of body and bounce.

Deer Repellent

Are deer destroying your garden? Drape a few Slinkys around the perimeter of the garden. That trademark "Slinkity" sound will scare those pesky deer back to Bambiville where they belong.

Slinky Sculpture

Use a Slinky as your wire base, then coat with strips of cloth soaked in Plaster of Paris to make a life-size Slinky.

Chimney Topper

Birds flying down your chimney? Stretch out a Slinky and wrap it into a tangled ball, then wedge it into your chimney top as a screen. WARNING: Remove the mass of metal knots from your chimney before Christmas Eve so Santa Claus isn't sliced and diced.

Christmas Clearance

Climb up on the roof of your house, hold one end of a Slinky and drop the other end down your chimney to make sure the coast is clear for Santa Claus. BONUS TIP: Instead of leaving a plate of cookies and milk for Santa like everyone else on your block, leave something Santa is sure to enjoy—a Slinky!

The Slinky in History #4

In 1776, General George Washington made crossing the Delaware River in the midst of a freezing cold winter more bearable by giving his troops Slinkys— an ingenious strategic move that catapulted him to the first presidency of the United States.

A Slinky Moment

Golden Spiral, a company based in Boulder Creek, Colorado, hooks two smooth, colored plastic funnels together with a fine metal coil made from high-grade piano wire. They call their invention the SpacePhone—"Alexander Graham Bell meets the Slinky!"

Slinky Pencil Holder

Standing a Slinky on your office desk to hold
your pens and pencils will make a statement
the corporate world will never forget.

Cookie Cutter

A Slinky is just the right diameter to cut cookies from a
rolled sheet of chocolate chip dough. Bonus Tip: In a dire
emergency, you can also use a Slinky as a somewhat
effective rolling pin.

Slinky Trellis

Hang several Slinkys in a row from the side of the house
or an overhang to give bean plants or grape vines a trellis
to slink their way up.

The Slinky Derby

Place ten Slinkys at the top of a wide staircase, have your
friends place their bets, and then race the Slinkys to the
bottom. Will Slinky races ever become an Olympic sport?
Send those letters to the U.S. Olympic Committee.

Dog Shield

If a mad dog is chasing after you, swing a Slinky like a lasso around your head to scare it away.

Found Money

Lose a coin down a drain? Attach a piece of chewed-up bubble gum to one end of a Slinky and, holding the other end, lower the spring toy down the drain. One tug on the Slinky and the coin will spring into your hand.

Cool Key Chain

Attach your keys to one end of a Slinky Junior and slip the other end onto your belt to make a key chain that easily stretches to any lock within reach.

Home on the Range

Tired of having to shell out good money for a bucket of golf balls at the driving range? Attach a golf ball to a Slinky so you can practice your golf swing to your heart's content. WARNING: Protective helmet and body gear strongly advised.

Size Matters

Place a Slinky and a Slinky Junior at the top of a staircase. Flip the top coil of each Slinky to the next lower step and let go. Which Slinky will win a race down the stairs? Why?

How fast a Slinky walks down steps depends on how quickly a longitudinal wave travels through the Slinky coil. And that depends on the tension and mass of the coil. The tighter the tension, the faster the longitudinal wave travels through the coil. The smaller the mass of the Slinky, the tighter the tension in the coil. The wave moves faster through the smaller Slinky, making it travel quicker.

Love at First Slinky

Attach one end of a Slinky to a tennis ball, the other end to your tennis racket. Now your serves will always be returned.

Practice Your Pitch

Having trouble finding a catcher to practice your baseball pitching? Fear not. Just attach one end of a Slinky to the baseball, the other end to your baseball mitt. Now you can pitch the ball over home plate and catch it, too.

'Tis the Season

To create a homemade Christmas wreath, wrap a Slinky around an old bicycle tire and secure the ends of the Slinky together with a twist-tie. Then decorate the Slinky with small branches of pine needles, little bells, red ribbon, and seasonal knickknacks. Slinky all the way!

The Amazing Slinky Game

Challenge friends to flip a Slinky! Roll a ball through an out-stretched Slinky! See who can make a Slinky walk down the most stairs! With six different  activities easy enough for a six-year-old, the Amazing Slinky Game guarantees hours of family fun. Two players race around the board competing in Slinky events. The Amazing Slinky Game is available at toy stores everywhere, or visit University Games at www.ugames.com.

High Wire Safety

Now you can walk the high wire in complete confidence.

Attach one end of the Slinky to your ankle, the other end to the high wire. If you fall off, you'll spring right back into place and the show can go on.

CD Organizer

Got no place to store your CD collection? Stretch out a Slinky and place a CD case between each coil.

Airport Insecurity

Want to make the airport security officers working the X-ray machine search your luggage? Pack a Slinky in your carry-on bag. BONUS TIP: If you'd like to be strip-searched, just wear two Slinky Juniors like crisscrossed bullet sashes under your clothes.

Slinky Fact

Slinkys adorn lighting fixtures in Harrah's Casino in Las Vegas because the interior designers like the unusual shadows the Slinkys cast.

See How They Run

Got a mouse in the house? When you see the little fellow, stretch a Slinky across the floor and drag the coils toward the uninvited house pest, directing the rodent to the nearest exit.

Practical Jokers!

Make rattling pipes even worse by wrapping a stretched-out Slinky around the pipes to magnify the clanking and clanging. This harmless little trick is guaranteed to drive your victim crazy.

Extension Cord Organizer

Fanfold an extension cord and store neatly inside a Slinky Junior.

Boot Tree

Insert a Slinky into each boot to help them keep their shape.

The Slinky in History #5

Frédéric-Auguste Bartholdi's first sketch of the Statue of Liberty depicted Lady Liberty playing with everyone's favorite toy—the ultimate symbol of freedom.

Car Security

Why use an expensive Club to lock your steering wheel in place? Simply wrap a Slinky around the steering wheel to totally baffle car thieves.

Chandelier Make-Over

With some Slinky Juniors you can redecorate that gaudy chandelier in your dining room to turn it into an artistic masterpiece.

Slinky Barbecue

Stand a Slinky in the middle of your barbecue grill, fill it with charcoal, add lighter fluid, and light on fire. When the coals glow, remove the Slinky with tongs and set it in a safe place. Bonus Tip: If you're feeling ambitious, you can use the red hot Slinky to brand cattle.

Slinky Juggling

Instead of juggling chainsaws or lit torches, try juggling Slinkys—the ultimate challenge.

Slinky Fact

Physical therapists sometimes prescribe a Slinky to their patients for coordination development.

Say Cheese!

In a pinch, you can use a Slinky as a cheese grater. All it takes is a hunk of cheese, a little determination, and a lot of desperation.

Slide 'n' Return

Attach one end of a Slinky to the top of a sliding board, the other end to the back of your belt. Now you can go down the slide time and time again without the constant ordeal of climbing up the ladder.

Loose Cannons

Tired of losing all those cannonballs? Attach one end of a Slinky to the cannonball, the other end to the inside of your cannon, and you'll never have to replace those cannonballs again. They hit the target, then reload into your cannon all by themselves.

Body Piercing

If you enjoy wearing pieces of metal through your body, why not go all the way? There's nothing quite as attention-getting as a Slinky pierced through your tongue. And it also makes eating an exciting challenge!

Hook, Line, and Sinker

Attach a hook and sinker to one end of a Slinky, bait the hook, and holding the other end, toss the Slinky into a lake or sea. Sure, casting is a bit difficult, but the harder the fish tries to get away, the easier it is for you to reel in the catch.

Climb Any Mountain

Instead of carrying all that cumbersome climbing gear, use a Slinky to attach mountain climbers to each other. This way, if someone falls down the side of the mountain, they'll bounce right back up.

Anchors Away

Hello sailor! Attach one end of a Slinky to the anchor, the other end to the boat, and lower the anchor to the bottom of the sea. Now raising the anchor will be a snap!

Coiled Again!

Foil a bicycle thief! Instead of using a bulky cable, run the coils of a Slinky through the frame and wheels of your  bicycle and around a sturdy post, then padlock the two end loops at the end of the Slinky together. Best of all, when you unlock the bike, the Slinky compacts.

Low-Budget Special Effects

Just because you're an amateur photographer doesn't mean you can't get professional results! Hold the center of a Slinky over the lens of a camera and stretch the Slinky out so you're taking photos through the telescoping coils. It's surreal!

Perpetual Motion

In a department store, walk onto an Up escalator, set a Slinky on the step behind you, and, halfway up the escalator, flip the top coil of the Slinky to the next lower step so the Slinky starts walking down the stairs of the escalator. If the escalator moves at the same speed as the Slinky, the Slinky will continue walking down the escalator forever.

WARNING: Other shoppers riding the escalator may create an obstacle for your Slinky, and walking down an Up escalator to stay with your Slinky may prompt store security officers to forcibly remove you from the premises.

Get on the Ball

Hold one end of a Slinky in the air, the other end on the ground, then drop a Ping-Pong ball through the top of the Slinky without letting the ball fall through the slats of the Slinky. It's fun for the entire family!

Slinky-Vision

Instead of hanging a traditional mobile over your baby's crib, attach several Slinkys to a wooden dowel to make a bouncing Slinky mobile that's sure to keep any bouncing baby amused for hours.

Get Wired

Secure stereo speaker wires, phone wires, and extension cords together behind furniture by running them through several plastic Slinkys. WARNING: Never use metal Slinkys to secure electrical wiring together unless you're determined to electrocute yourself, short out your fuse box, blow up your television, and possibly burn your house to the ground.

In this self-portrait painted in 1888, Vincent van Gogh bounces back with refreshing humor after cutting off his ear to win the affection of a woman.

Beautiful Legs

Hold two bridge tables together by setting each pair of adjacent table legs inside a Slinky. You can let the Slinky sit on the floor, or stretch the Slinky up the two legs of the table for a trendier look.

Slinky "Basketball"

Hang a Slinky on the wall and let the rest of the coil drop to the floor. Toss a tennis ball or Ping-Pong ball at the open Slinky hoop to get a basket. The ball will then roll down the Slinky shoot and return to you. With a little practice, you'll be on your way to the NBA in no time.

Slinky Golf

Lie a Slinky on its side on the carpeted floor of your home or office and—*presto change-o!*—you've got a challenging indoor golf course. How do you think Tiger Woods got his start? BONUS TIP: For a greater golf challenge, stretch the Slinky across the floor into a long, curving tube and try to hit the ball through it.

Tree Protector

Tired of scarring young trees and plants
when mowing the lawn? Hang a Slinky
around the trunk of that young tree or plant,
mow the grass around it, then slip off the Slinky
and put it on the next tree.

Flower Power

Troubled by flowers that just won't stay
together in a vase? Insert all the stems
through the center of a Slinky Junior
before placing the flowers inside the
vase, and your flower troubles will be
gone forever!

Blowing in the Wind

Hang five Slinky Juniors together from a small block of
wood to create an attractive Slinky wind chime that will
make music to your ears and make all your neighbors
green with envy.

What They Really Meant to Say

"To Slinky or not to Slinky, that is the question."
—William Shakespeare

"A Slinky saved is a Slinky earned."
—Benjamin Franklin

"Give me a Slinky or give me death."
—Patrick Henry

"All Slinkys are created equal."
—Abraham Lincoln

"Workers of the world unite!
You have nothing to lose but your Slinkys."
—Karl Marx

"Walk softly and carry a big Slinky."
—Theodore Roosevelt

"God does not play Slinky with the universe."
—Albert Einstein

"A Slinky is a Slinky is a Slinky."
—Gertrude Stein

"The Slinky stops here."
—Harry Truman

"Ask not what your Slinky can do for you,
but what you can do for your Slinky."
—John F. Kennedy

"I have a Slinky."
—Martin Luther King

"That's one small Slinky for man, one giant Slinky for mankind."
—Neil Armstrong

Swing 'n' Sway

Hang a planter from the awning or ceiling of your house with a Slinky to give your plants eternal spring.

Slinky through the Grapevine

Build a simple wood frame with legs and drape a dozen Slinkys across it so grapevines can grow around the coils. Now you've got your own vineyard!

Umbrella Holster

Slip a folded umbrella inside a Slinky Junior for safekeeping. BONUS TIP: Opening the umbrella without removing the Slinky will send the spring toy sky-rocketing.

Houseguest Repellent

Stretch Slinkys across couches and chairs to prevent uninvited guests from sitting down. WARNING: Uninvited guests may play with the Slinkys and never leave.

Slinky in Training

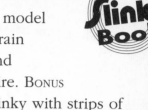

A Slinky makes a great tunnel for that model railroad. Just slip the HO- or N-scale train track through the center of a Slinky and stretch the coils to the length you desire. BONUS TIP: For a realistic tunnel, cover the Slinky with strips of newspaper soaked in Plaster of Paris, let dry, and paint.

Off Limits

Stretch a neon-colored plastic Slinky between two trees or lamp posts to make a barricade for emergency situations (and lighten up the tense atmosphere at an otherwise humorless crime scene).

Parking Made Slinky

Tired of smashing your car into the garage wall? Secure a Slinky to the ceiling of the garage and let it hang down to touch the front bumper of your car so you know exactly where to stop the car when you park.

Slinky Fact

United States soldiers using radios during combat in Vietnam tossed the Slinky into trees to act as a makeshift antenna.

Slinky Hair-do

Slip a long braid of hair through a stretched
Slinky Junior and secure the Slinky in place
by tying a bow at the top and bottom of the
braid. Now you're a Space-age Pollyanna!

Meter Beater

Do you hate putting money in parking meters? Using
epoxy glue, attach several Slinky Juniors to a parking meter
to make the devilish device appear completely "out of
order."

Prowler Fouler

Hang Slinkys over the drainpipes on the sides of your
house so cat burglars can't climb up them—without making
enough noise to wake up the entire neighborhood.

Belt Loopy

A Slinky makes a fashionable belt. And for an added touch
of class, you can use a padlock for a belt buckle (just don't
lose the key or forget the combination).

Get a Little Tail

Stuff a Slinky Junior with crumpled-up sheets of newspaper, insert the Slinky into a cut-off leg of a pair of black panty hose, and attach with safety pins to the back of a costume for a convincing tail.

Slinky Snake

Make an enormous serpent by stuffing a Slinky with crumpled-up sheets of newspaper. Then cut off the legs from a pair of black panty hose and slip the stuffed Slinky inside. Use two buttons for eyes and add a piece of red felt for a forked tongue.

Adorable Adornment

Can't find the "Do Not Disturb" sign? Hang a Slinky on the doorknob to leave housekeeping personnel completely baffled.

That Slinkity Sound

The original Slinky jingle described the sound a Slinky makes as "slinkity." There are dozens of ways to make music to everyone's ears with a Slinky and a little ingenuity:

• Stretch a Slinky across the room and hit the coils with xylophone sticks.

• Hold the end of a Slinky in each hand and play the Slinky like a pair of cymbals.

• String a cello with Slinky Juniors.

• Place a Slinky in a trash compactor, then switch it on for an impressive symphony of *springs*, *sprangs*, and *sproings*.

• Climb up into the steeple of your local church and replace the clappers in the bells with Slinkys. If you're feeling more ambitious, fly to Paris and replace the clappers in the bells at the Cathedral of Notre Dame.

L'chaim!

Rebellious Hasidic Jews can use two Slinky Juniors to simulate *payess* rather than growing the traditional long ringlets of hair from the temples. WARNING: While Slinkys do not contain any pork or shellfish, they are not manufactured under rabbinic supervision.

To Protect and Plant

Protect plants in your garden with Slinkys. Pushing Slinkys into the soil around young tomatoes, potatoes, and pepper plants will fend off cutworms, grubs, and other pests. The Slinkys will also shelter the sprouting plants from the wind.

Birds of a Feather

Attach a worm to one end of a Slinky and stake the other end of the Slinky to the ground. The early bird may get the worm, but it won't be able to fly very far away with it!

The Slinky in History #7

Michelangelo's marble sculpture of David, on display in Florence, Italy, captures the young hero offering to share his Slinky with Goliath.

Corn on the Cob Protector

Slip a cooked cob of corn through a Slinky to prevent your dinner guests from digging in until everyone sits down to the table.

Bumper Stumper

Do you keep smashing the vacuum cleaner into the legs of the dining room table? Place furniture legs inside Slinkys to avoid bumping into furniture when vacuuming. Or better yet, attach plastic Slinkys to the front of your vacuum cleaner so it bounces right off any furniture you accidentally hit.

A Slinky Moment

Based on the original Slinky design,
a plastic Glow-in-the-Dark Slinky can be
seen in a pitch-black room for all your
glow-in-the-dark needs.

Anti-Smoking Device

A Slinky is a great tranquilizer for someone who has just quit smoking. Bouncing a Slinky between your hands steadies the nerves. WARNING: The Surgeon General has determined that playing with a Slinky may be habit forming.

Rattle a Rattlesnake

Feed a Slinky to a rattlesnake and have hours of educational fun watching the coils go through the snake's body as it tries to digest the impossible and gets completely rattled.

The Eyes Have It

Never lose your eyeglasses again. Use a Slinky as an eyeglass strap. This way, if your glasses fall off, they'll spring right back into place.

Slinky Fact

The Slinky helps scientists understand the supercoiling of DNA molecules. Slinky and Shear Slinky, two computer graphics programs developed at the University of Maryland, use a Slinky model to approximate the double helix coiling of DNA molecules.

A Slinky Wedding

Miniature Slinkys would make great wedding bands that would truly capture the romantic spirit of matrimony, the flexibility required by both partners for a successful marriage, and the shared intimacy of the bed spring. Now all we have to do is convince the Slinky Company to make them!

The Royal Slinky

If Queen Elizabeth really wants to be treated like royalty, she should ditch that pretentious golden crown garishly imbedded with diamonds and put on a crown fashioned from a Slinky.

Stop Thief!

There's only one sure-fire way to stop art thieves from stealing valuable paintings from the world's museums. Attach those art treasures to the museum walls with Slinkys so that if someone tries to take a masterpiece off the wall, the painting will spring right back into position.

Cattle Call

Tired of the monotonous sound of cow bells?
Transform your dairy farm into a delightful
musical menagerie by hanging a Slinky
around each cow's neck.

TV Guideline

Never misplace the TV program guide again. Anchor one
end of a Slinky to the television set, the other end to your
TV program guide. Now you'll always know what's on TV.
The TV program guide, of course.

Leak Silencer

Is the *kerplunk kerplunk kerplunk* of a leaky faucet keeping you up all night? Hang one end of a Slinky around the
faucet nozzle and let the other end drop into the drain.
The water will silently slide down the coils into the drain.
(Of course, you could call a plumber, but that would take
all the fun out of life.)

Barbie Doll Death Trap

Stretch a Slinky across the room and shove Barbie, Skipper, and Ken inside the coils.

Now they'll never get back to Barbie's Dream House—without help from G.I. Joe and Action Jackson.

Ball and Chain

Tired of dragging a ball and chain through the prison yard? Ask the warden to replace the chain with a Slinky. Simply weld one end of the Slinky to the steel ball, and secure the other end to your leg. Now that ball will follow after you with ease. WARNING: Walk slowly, otherwise the steel ball may be propelled back at you, knocking you over like a bowling pin.

Room Divider

Tired of sharing your room with a pesky brother or sister? Mark off your side of the room by stretching a Slinky down the middle of the room. WARNING: Be sure to give both parties access to the door.

The Slinky Workout

Less expensive and more versatile than the Thigh-Master, the Slinky is a 7-in-1 workout miracle machine!

➡ **Build Bulging Biceps!** Hold one end of a Slinky in each hand, raise your arms over your head, and stretch your arms apart and back together again for ten rounds.

➡ **Develop Muscular Shoulders!**

Close a door on one end of a Slinky to hold it in place, stand ten feet from the door, turn your back to the door, and holding the Slinky in your hand, stretch your arm forward and back for twenty rounds.

The Slinky Workout

➡ **Tighten Your Tummy!** Lie on the ground, slip your feet through the end coil of two Slinkys and, holding the other ends of the Slinky in your hands, do a round of fifty sit-ups.

➡ **Develop Chest Muscles!**
Hold one end of a Slinky in each hand in front of your chest, extend your arms out to your sides as far as you can, then return your hands to the front of your chest for ten rounds.

➡ **Broaden Your Back!**
Hold the end coils of a Slinky in each hand behind your back, stretch your arms out to your sides as far as you can, then return your hands to your sides for twenty rounds.

The Slinky Workout

➡ **Strengthen Your Wrists!** Hold each end of a Slinky with both hands, then quickly raise and lower each hand in a rhythmic motion for ten minutes.

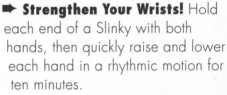

➡ **Tighten Your Abdomen!** Slip the Slinky between your legs, hold one end of the Slinky in front of you, the other end of the Slinky behind your back, and lift your arms to shoulder height for twenty rounds.

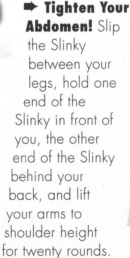

Bed Divider

Forced to share a motel bed with someone
you detest? Stretch a Slinky down the middle
of the bed to prevent either of you from
accidentally rolling onto the other side of the bed in
the middle of the night.

Napkin Leash

Does your napkin perpetually fall off your lap?
Tired of picking it up from the floor? Attach
one end of a Slinky Junior to the
napkin, the other end to your belt
loop, and never be without good
manners again.

Slinky Flamingo

Turn those pink flamingos on
your front lawn into a class act
by slipping Slinkys over their
legs. Now they're pink flamingos
from Mars!

The Slinky in History #8

During World War II, Allied fighter pilots struck fear into the heart of the Axis powers by securing one end of a Slinky to a bomb, the other end to the hatch doors of their bomber plane. This way, they could scare the pants off the enemy without causing any damage or casualties—saving billions of defense dollars and millions of lives.

Slinky Fact

In 1985, Space Shuttle astronaut Jeffrey Hoffman became the first person to play with a Slinky in zero-gravity physics experiments in orbit around the earth.

Platter Chatter

Chopped celery, carrots, cauliflower, and broccoli look much more elegant on a party platter when they're wrapped in Slinkys. And your guests are sure to comment!

Toilet Troubles

Wrap a Slinky into a huge tangled ball and shove it into a toilet bowl to confuse future bathroom visitors.

A Thanksgiving Treat

Cook a couple of Slinky Juniors inside the holiday turkey (with all the stuffing) for a Thanksgiving surprise the family will be talking about for years to come.

The Wild Winnebago

Instead of using a traditional trailer hitch, attach that trailer to your car with a Slinky. Now that trip across the Rocky Mountains will be an adventure your family will never forget.

Slinky Fact

Every Slinky ever produced has been made on the original machinery in the tiny town of Hollidaysburg, Pennsylvania.

Steps to Greatness

Here are the most challenging staircases in the world to walk a Slinky:

Leaning Tower of Pisa
Pisa, Italy
294 steps

Pyramid of Kukulcán
Chichén Itzá, Mexico
91 steps

Parthenon
Athens, Greece
12 steps

Spanish Steps
Rome, Italy
137 steps

Pyramid of the Sun
Teotihuacán, Mexico
248 steps

Great Pyramid of Cheops
Giza, Egypt
143 meters high

United States Capitol
Building
Washington, D.C.
117 steps

Lincoln Memorial
Washington, D.C.
58 steps

Waterskiing Tricks

Waterskiing is much more challenging when you use a Slinky in place of a traditional rope towline. Jump the wake the right way and you may just wind up back in the boat!

Pin the Slinky on the Donkey

Give your next game of "Pin the Tail on the Donkey" a little more zest by using Slinkys instead of those cheap paper tails.

Pen Protection

Tired of customers running off with your ballpoint pen? Attach one end of a Slinky to the pen and the other end to the desk top, and they'll always bounce right back into place.

Just Married

Instead of tying empty beer and soda cans to the back of the newlywed couple's getaway car, attach Slinkys for a farewell they'll never forget.

Slinky Fact

Since a Slinky can be stretched twenty-five feet without being stretched out of shape, you would need 50,446,599 Slinkys stretched end-to-end to reach the moon.

Slinky Hollywood

What They Should Have Said in the Movies

"Bring me the Slinky of the Wicked Witch of the West."
—The Wizard of Oz

"Of all the Slinkys in all the towns in all the world, she had to play with mine."
—Rick in *Casablanca*

"Frankly Scarlet, I don't give a Slinky."
—Rhett Butler

"Give him a Slinky he can't refuse."
—The Godfather

"May the Slinky be with you."
—Luke Skywalker

"E.T. play Slinky."
—E.T.

A Slinky Moment

James Industries issued a limited edition Slinky in a special reprint of the original Slinky box to celebrate the fiftieth anniversary of the Slinky.

Slinky Fact

A 1990 national survey revealed that nine out of ten Americans know what a Slinky is.

The Slinky in History #9

A Slinky walks down the steps of the Lunar Module to join Neil Armstrong and Buzz Aldrin as the first toy on the moon, winning the space race against the Yo-Yo, Silly Putty, and the Frisbee.

Slinky Safety Tips

■ Do not store a Slinky alone in a dark, empty shoebox. Slinkys must be stored with other Slinkys, otherwise they become very lonely and depressed. (WARNING: Storing two Slinkys alone together in a shoebox may result in a box full of Slinky Juniors.)

■ Do not store a Slinky in a garbage can sitting on the curb of your street.

■ Do not play with a Slinky while you are strapped into an electric chair—unless you are determined to black out a major metropolitan area.

■ Do not throw a Slinky into an active volcano in the hope of preventing an impending eruption.

■ Do not try to make a Slinky walk up a staircase.

For more fun with Slinky
and to share your wild and wacky uses
for the world's greatest toy,
visit Joey Green on the internet at
http://www.wackyuses.com/slinky

Acknowledgments

I am gratefully indebted to the wonderful people at James Industries, Inc., for graciously opening their hearts and the Slinky archives to let this Slinky Book spring forth: Ray Dallavecchia, Betty James, and Tom James. My editor, Hillary Cige, championed the Slinky cause at Penguin Putnam, and my agent, Jeremy Solomon at First Books, was once again as quick and nimble as a Slinky walking down a staircase. Thanks also go out to Christine Zika, Grace Paik, Lisa Vitelli, and Peggy Cohen. Above all, I love Debbie, Ashley, and Julia for always being willing to race Slinkys down the stairs.

Photo credits: James Industries, Inc.: pages viii, xiii; Joey Green: pages ix, 17, 23, 55, 57, 67, 91-93, 99-101; Photo collages by Joey Green: pages 19, 31, 39 (from *Proportions of Man* by Leonardo da Vinci), 51 (from *Crossing the Delaware* by Emanuel Leutze), 69 (from *Self-Portrait* by Vincent van Gogh), 83, 95 (from U.S. Air Force photo), 107 (from NASA photo).

About the Author

Joey Green is the bestselling author of many books, including *Polish Your Furniture with Panty Hose* and *Wash Your Hair with Whipped Cream*. He has made guest appearances on *The Rosie O'Donnell Show, The Tonight Show with Jay Leno,* and *Late Night with Conan O'Brien,* and has been  profiled in *People* magazine and *The New York Times.* He lives in Los Angeles with his wife, Debbie, and their daughters, Ashley and Julia.